STEP ONE:

Play Guitar Chords

by Len Vogler

200 essential chords in all twelve keys, fully fingered, in standard notation and handy chord diagrams. A complete resource for the beginning guitarist.

Gibson Johnny Smith pictured on cover owned by Scot Arch
Photographed by William H. Draffen

This book Copyright © 1997 by Amsco Publications,
A Division of Music Sales Corporation, New York

Order No. AM 943151
US International Standard Book Number: 0.8256.1609.3
UK International Standard Book Number: 0.7119.6479.3

Exclusive Distributors:
Music Sales Corporation
257 Park Avenue South, New York, NY 10010 USA
Music Sales Limited
8/9 Frith Street, London W1V 5TZ England
Music Sales Pty. Limited
120 Rothschild Street, Rosebery, Sydney, NSW 2018, Australia

Printed in the United States of America by
Vicks Lithograph and Printing Corporation

Amsco Publications
New York/London/Sydney

CD Track List

Contents

Chord Construction

Scales

In order to talk about chord structure we need to discuss the foundation by which chords are formed—*scales*. There are a multitude of scales available to the musician, but we will explain only those that are most pertinent—the major, minor, and chromatic scales.

Major

I   II   III   IV   V   VI   VII   VIII   VII   VI   *etc.*

Harmonic minor

I   II   III   IV   V   VI   VII   VIII   VII   VI   *etc.*

Melodic minor

I   II   III   IV   V   VI   VII   VIII   VII   VI   *etc.*

Chromatic

Scales are determined by the distribution of *half steps* and *whole steps*. For example, the major scale has half steps between scale steps three and four, and between seven and eight. The harmonic minor has half steps between scale steps two and three, five and six, and seven and eight. The melodic minor scale's ascending order finds half steps between scale steps two and three, and between seven and eight. Descending, the half steps fall between scale steps six and five, and between three and two; and a whole step is now in place between eight and seven.

It is common to refer to scale steps, or *degrees*, by Roman numerals as in the example above and also by the following names:

I. Tonic
II. Supertonic
III. Mediant
IV. Subdominant
V. Dominant
VI. Submediant
VII. Leading tone

Intervals

An *interval* is the distance between two notes. This is the basis for harmony (chords). The naming of intervals, as in the example below, is fairly standard, but you may encounter other terminology in various forms of musical literature.

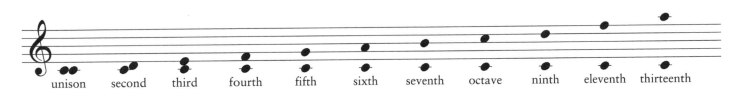

unison   second   third   fourth   fifth   sixth   seventh   octave   ninth   eleventh   thirteenth

Chords

Chords are produced by combining two or more intervals, and the simplest of these combinations is a *triad*. A triad consists of three notes obtained by the superposition of two thirds. The notes are called the *root*, the *third*, and the *fifth*.

Inversions

Inversions are produced by arranging the intervals of a chord in a different order. A triad that has the root as the bottom or lowest tone is said to be in *root position.* A triad with a third as the bottom or lowest tone is in *first inversion,* and a triad with a fifth as the bottom or lowest tone is in *second inversion.* As the chords become more complex—such as, sixths, sevenths, etc.—there will be more possible inversions.

root   first inversion   second inversion

Note that when inverting more complex chords the inversion may actually become a completely different chord.

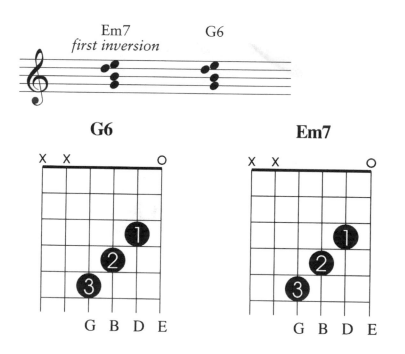

Altered Triads

When a chord consists of a root, major third, and a perfect fifth it is known as a *major triad.* When the triad is altered by lowering the major third one half-step, it becomes a *minor triad.* The examples below are chords that have altered intervals.

How to Use This Book

The Chord Diagram

The chords are displayed as diagrams that represent the fingerboard of the guitar. There are six vertical lines representing the six strings of the guitar. Horizontal lines represent the frets. The strings are arranged with the high E (first, or thinnest) string to the right, and the low E (sixth, or thickest) to the left. The black circles indicate at which fret the finger is to be placed and the number tells you which finger to use. At the top of the diagram there is a thick black line indicating the nut of the guitar. Diagrams for chords up the neck just have a fret line at the top with a Roman numeral to the right to identify the first fret of the diagram. Above the chord diagram you will occasionally see x's and o's. An x indicates that the string below it is either not played or damped, an o simply means the string is played as an open string. At the bottom of the diagram are the note names that make up the chord. This information can be helpful when making up lead licks or chord solos. A curved line tells you to bar the strings with the finger shown; that is, lay your finger flat across the indicated strings.

The fingerings in this book might be different from fingerings you have encountered in other chord books. They were chosen for their overall practicality in the majority of situations.

The Photo

The photo to right of each chord diagram shows you what your hand should look like on the guitar fingerboard. You will notice that the finger positions in some of the photos are a little to the right or left of the frame. This is done to show the particular chord form's proximity to either the twelfth fret or the nut of the guitar. This makes it easier to recognize the relative position on the fretboard at a glance.

Although the photos are a visual reference, all of the fingers in a given shot may not be in a proper playing position. We have sometimes moved unused fingers *out of the way,* to give you a better look at where the fretting fingers are placed. For instance, when playing the Absus4 shown in the photograph below, your second and third finger should not be tucked under the neck, they would be relaxed and extended upward over the fingerboard. Make sure your fingers are comfortable and that you are capable of moving them easily from one chord position to another.

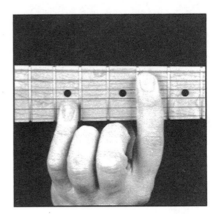

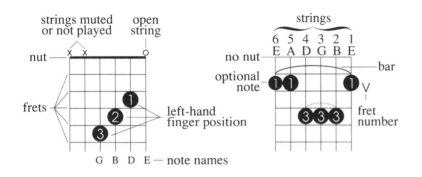

C chords

C major

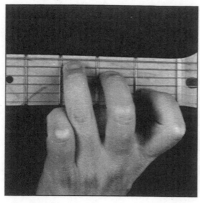

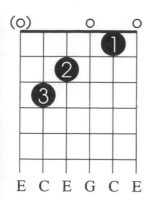

E C E G C E

C major

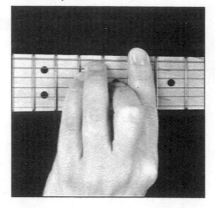

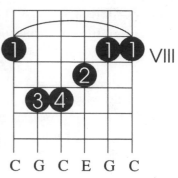

VIII

C G C E G C

Csus4

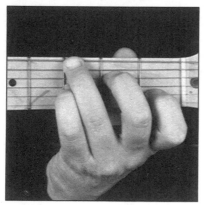

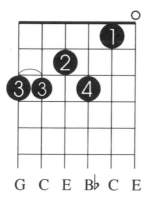

C F G C F

C6

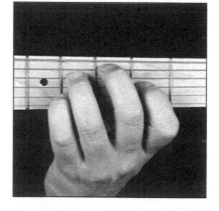

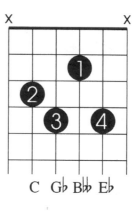

G E A C

C7

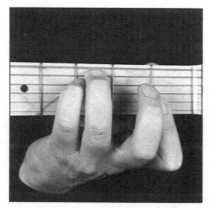

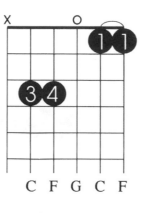

G C E B♭ C E

C°7

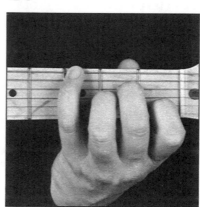

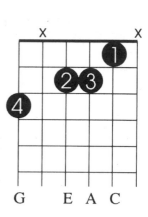

C G♭ B♭♭ E♭

C9

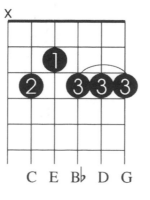

C E B♭ D G

C13

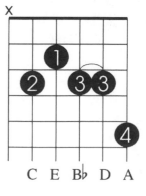

C E B♭ D A

8

Cmaj7

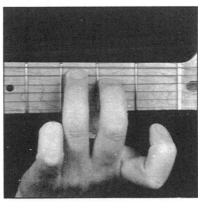

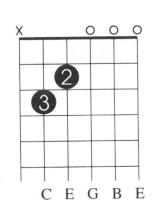

C E G B E

Cm7

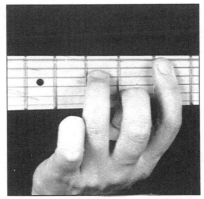

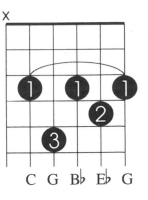

C G Bb Eb G

Cm

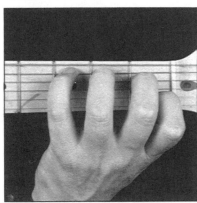

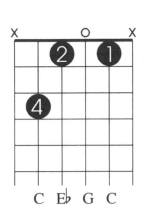

C Eb G C

Cm

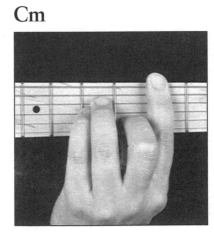

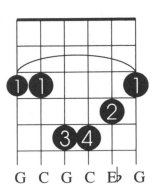

G C G C Eb G

Cm6

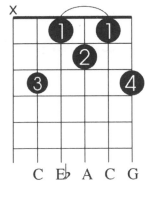

C Eb A C G

Cm7b5

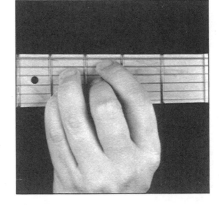

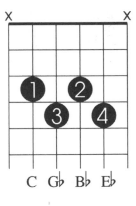

C Gb Bb Eb

Cm(maj7)

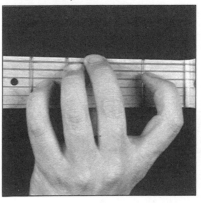

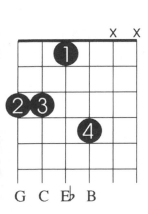

G C Eb B

Cm11

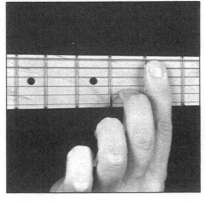

C F Bb Eb G

9

C#/Db chords

C# major

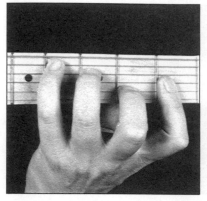

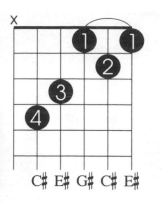

C# E# G# C# E#

C# major

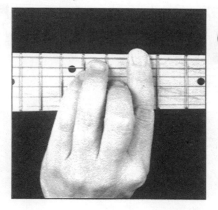

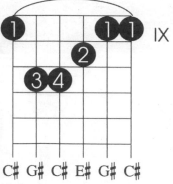

IX

C# G# C# E# G# C#

C#sus4

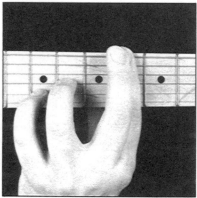

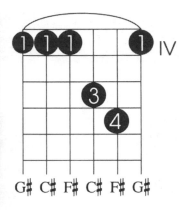

IV

G# C# F# C# F# G#

C#6

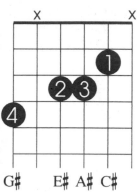

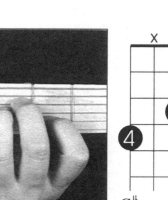

G# E# A# C#

C#7

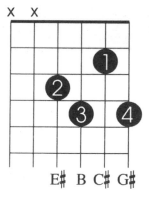

E# B C# G#

C#°7

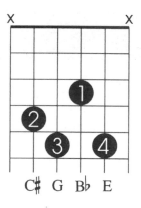

C# G Bb E

C#9

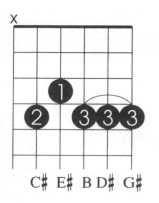

C# E# B D# G#

C#13

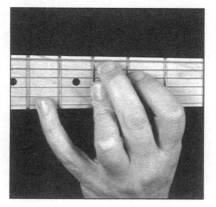

III

C# E# B D# A#

C#maj7

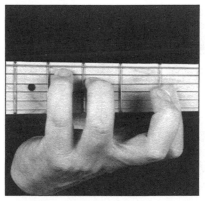
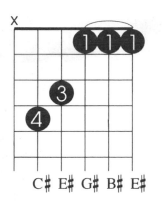

C# E# G# B# E#

C#m7

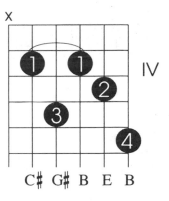

IV

C# G# B E B

C#m

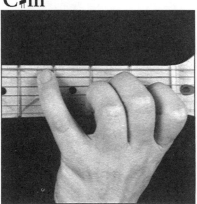
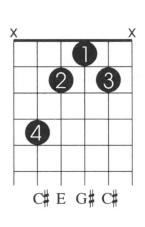

C# E G# C#

C#m

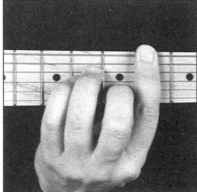
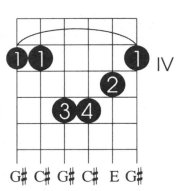

IV

G# C# G# C# E G#

C#m6

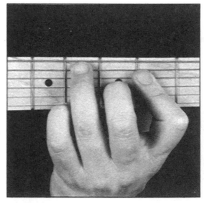
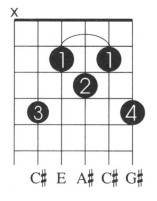

C# E A# C# G#

C#m7b5

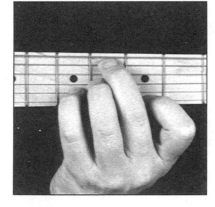
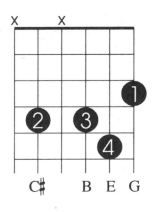

C# B E G

C#m(maj7)

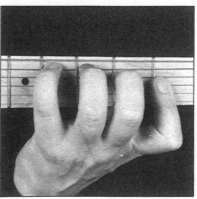
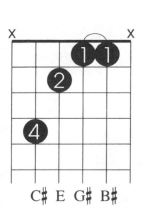

C# E G# B#

C#m11

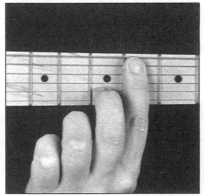
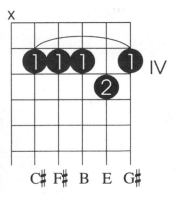

IV

C# F# B E G#

D chords

D major

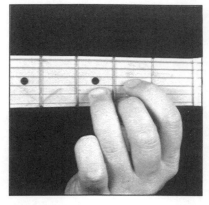

X O O

A D A D F#

D major

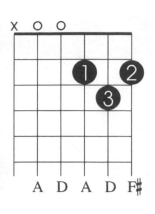

X

D A D F# A D

Dsus4

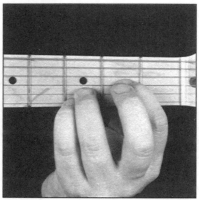

X X O

D A D G

D6

X O O O

A D A B F#

D7

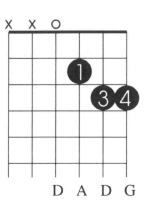

X O O

A D A C F#

D°7

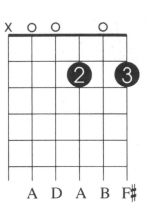

X X O O

D A♭ C♭ F

D9

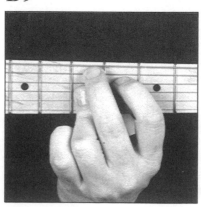

X

D F# C E A

D13

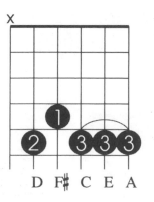

X

IV

D F# C E B

Dmaj7

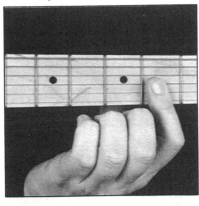
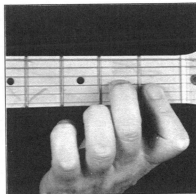

A D A C# F#

Dm7

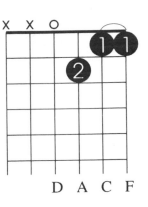

D A C F

Dm

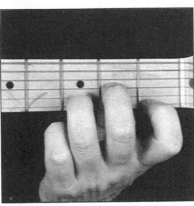
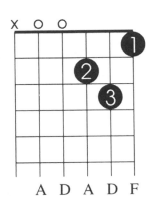

A D A D F

Dm

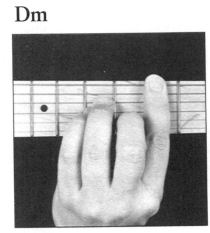

A D A D F A   V

Dm6

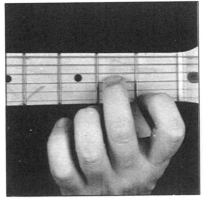

D A B F

Dm7♭5

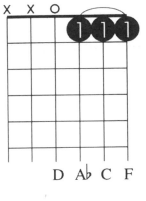

D A♭ C F

Dm(maj7)

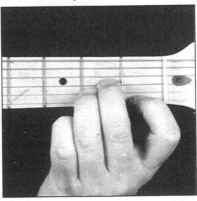

D A C# F

Dm11

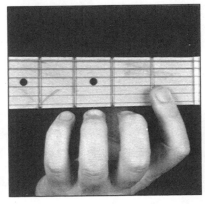
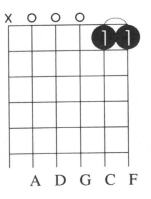

A D G C F

Eb/D♯ chords

Eb major

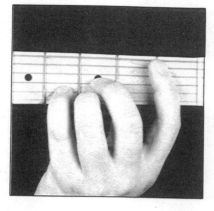

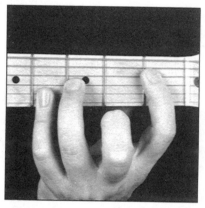

X

❶ ❶

② ③

④

Bb Eb Bb Eb G

VIII

Eb major

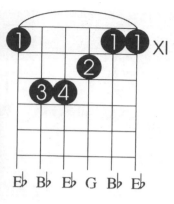

① ① ①

②

③ ④

XI

Eb Bb Eb G Bb Eb

Ebsus4

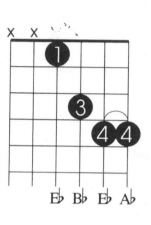

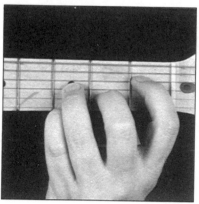

X X

①

③

④ ④

Eb Bb Eb Ab

Eb6

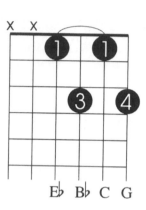

X X

① ①

③ ④

Eb Bb C G

Eb7

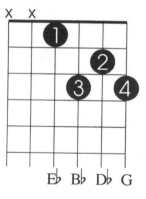

X X

①

②

③ ④

Eb Bb Db G

Eb°7

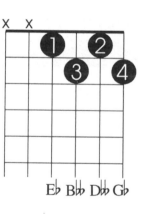

X X

① ②

③ ④

Eb Bbb Dbb Gb

Eb9

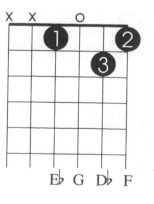

X X O

① ②

③

Eb G Db F

Eb13

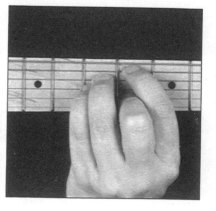

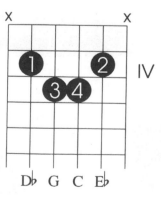

X X

① ②

③ ④

IV

Db G C Eb

E♭maj7

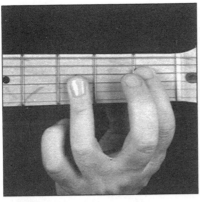

X X
1
3 3 3

E♭ B♭ D G

E♭m7

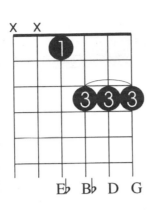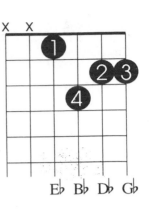

X X
1
2 3
4

E♭ B♭ D♭ G♭

E♭m

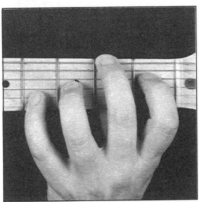

X · X
2 · 1
3
4

G♭ · E♭ B♭ E♭

E♭m

1 1 1 · 1 VI
2
3 4

B♭ E♭ B♭ E♭ G♭ B♭

E♭m6

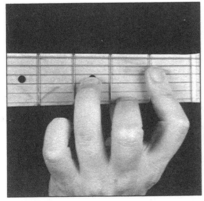

X X
1 1
2
3

E♭ B♭ C G♭

E♭m7♭5

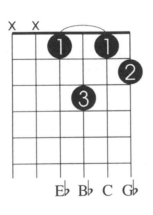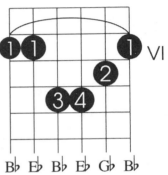

X X
1
3 3 3

E♭ B♭♭ D♭ G♭

E♭m(maj7)

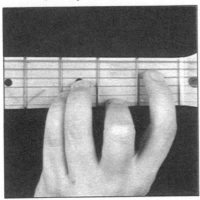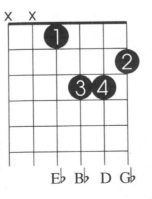

X X
1
2
3 4

E♭ B♭ D G♭

E♭m11

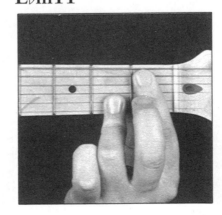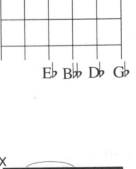

X
1 1 1
3 3

B♭ E♭ A♭ D♭ G♭

15

E chords

E major

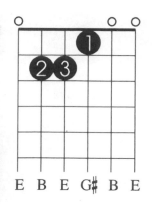

E B E G# B E

E major

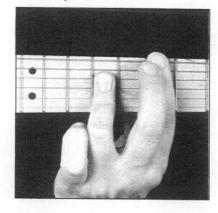

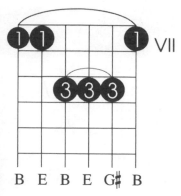

VII

B E B E G# B

Esus4

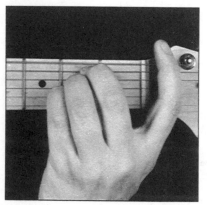

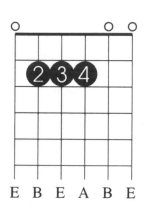

E B E A B E

E6

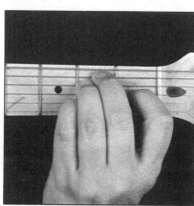

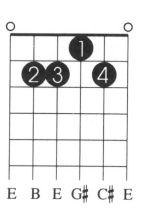

E B E G# C# E

E7

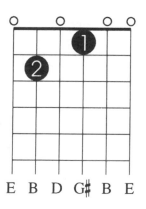

E B D G# B E

E°7

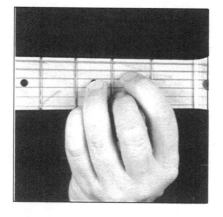

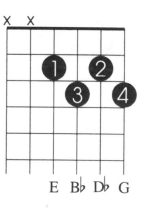

E Bb Db G

E9

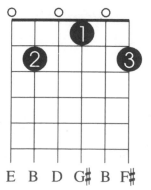

E B D G# B F#

E13

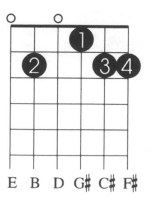

E B D G# C# F#

Emaj7

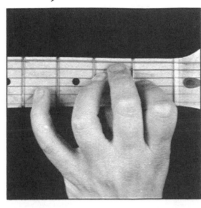
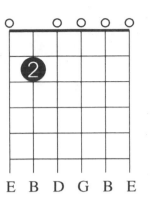

E B E G# D# E

Em7

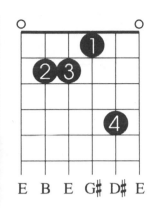

E B D G B E

Em

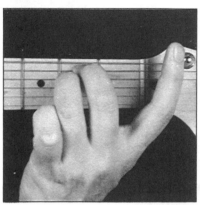
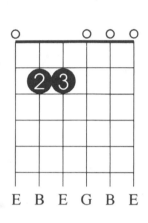

E B E G B E

Em

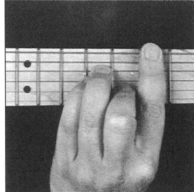
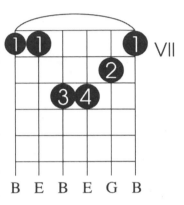

B E B E G B

Em6

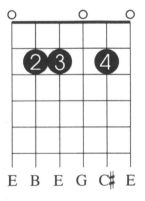

E B E G C# E

Em7b5

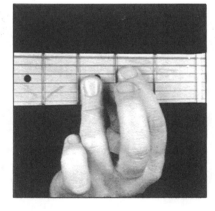
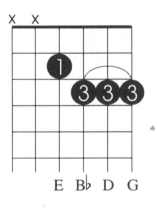

E Bb D G

Em(maj7)

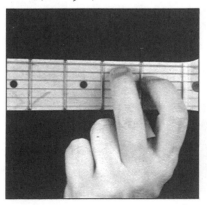
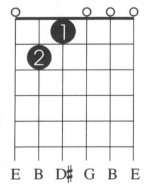

E B D# G B E

Em11

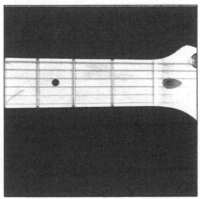

E A D G B E

F chords

F major

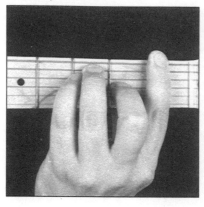
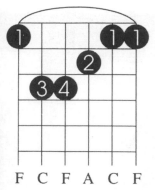

F C F A C F

F major

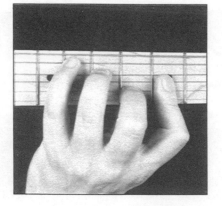
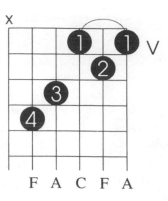

F A C F A

Fsus4

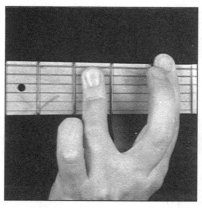
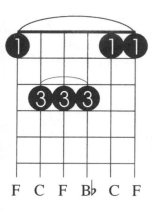

F C F B♭ C F

F6

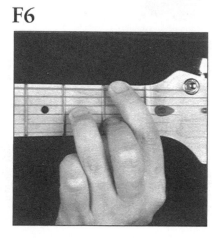
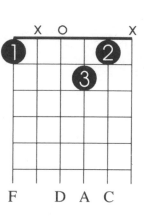

F D A C

F7

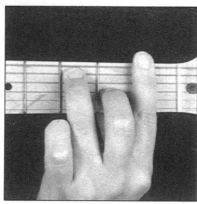
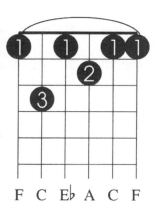

F C E♭ A C F

F°7

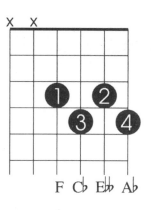

F C♭ E♭♭ A♭

F9

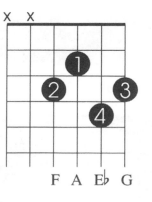

F A E♭ G

F13

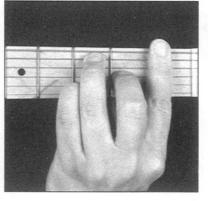

F C E♭ A D F

Fmaj7

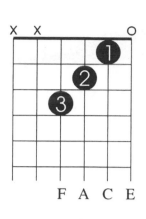

x   x   o

F   A   C   E

Fm7

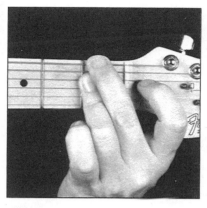

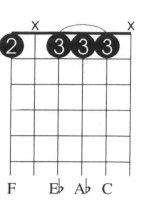

x

F   E♭ A♭ C

Fm

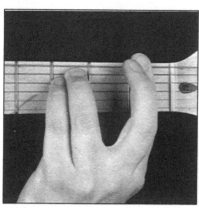

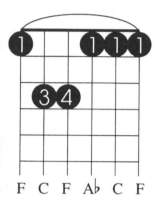

F   C   F   A♭ C   F

Fm

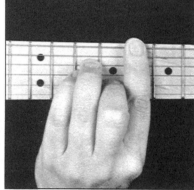

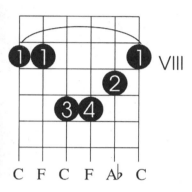

VIII

C   F   C   F   A♭ C

Fm6

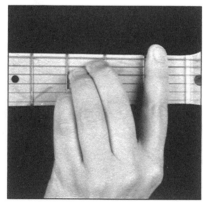

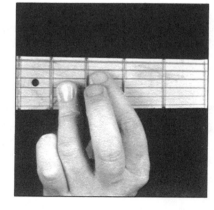

F   C   F   A♭ D   F

Fm7♭5

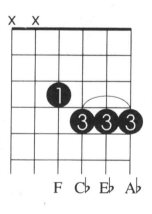

x   x

F   C♭ E♭ A♭

Fm(maj7)

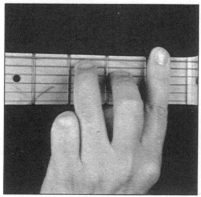

F   C   E   A♭ C   F

Fm11

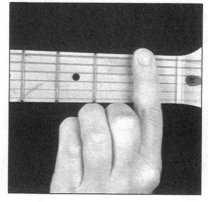

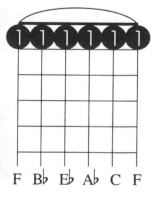

F   B♭ E♭ A♭ C   F

19

F#/Gb chords

F# major

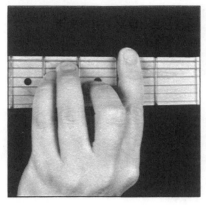

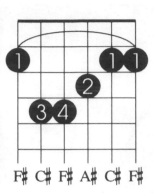

F# C# F# A# C# F#

F# major

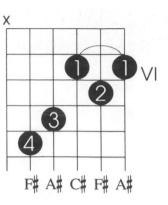

X

VI

F# A# C# F# A#

F#sus4

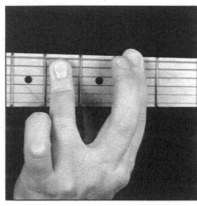

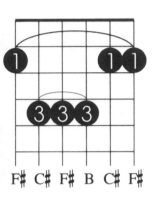

F# C# F# B C# F#

F#6

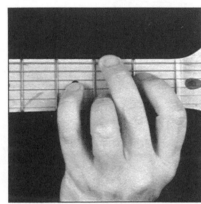

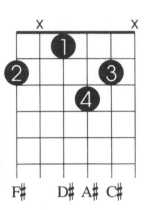

X   X

F#   D# A# C#

F#7

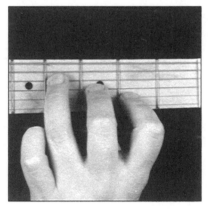

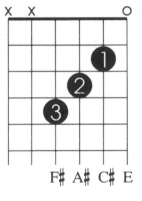

X X   O

F# A# C# E

F#°7

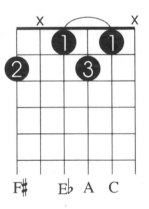

X   X

F#   Eb A   C

F#9

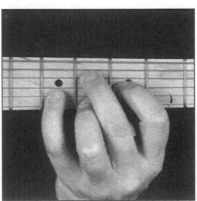

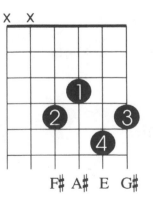

X X

F# A# E G#

F#13

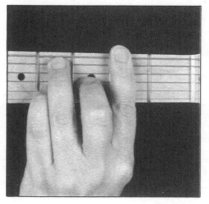

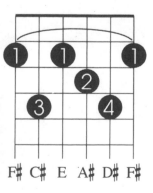

F# C# E A# D# F#

F#maj7

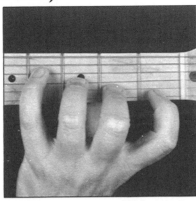

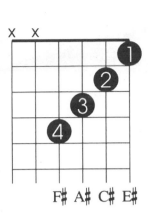

F# A# C# E#

F#m7

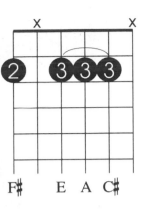

F# E A C#

F#m

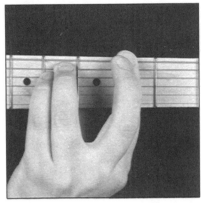

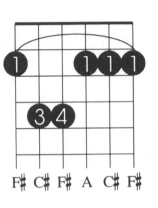

F# C# F# A C# F#

F#m

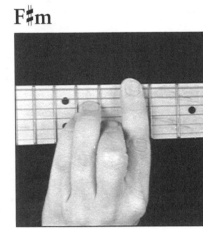

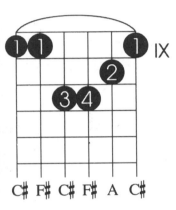

|X

C# F# C# F# A C#

F#m6

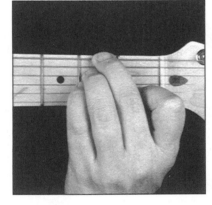

F# D# A C# F#

F#m7♭5

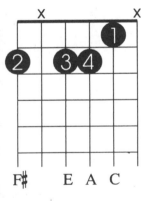

F# E A C

F#m(maj7)

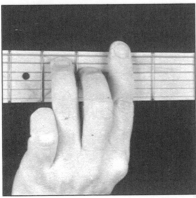

F# C# E# A C# F#

F#m11

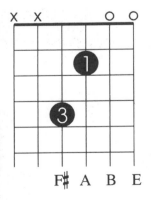

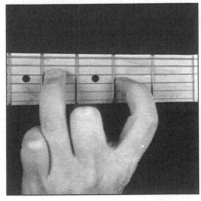

F# A B E

21

G chords

G major

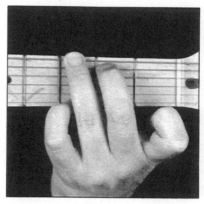
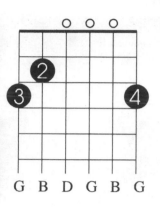

G B D G B G

G major

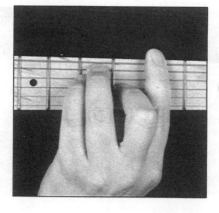
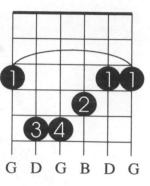

G D G B D G

Gsus4

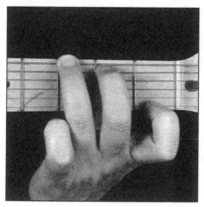
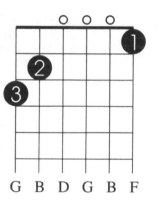

G D G C G

G6

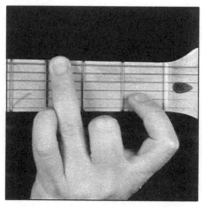
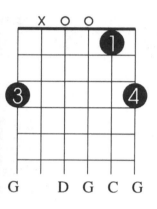

G B D G B E

G7

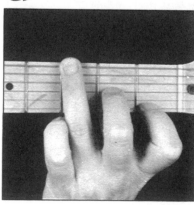
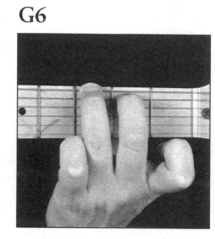

G B D G B F

G°7

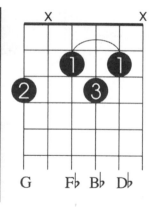
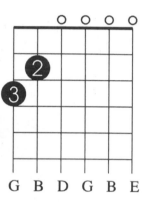

G F♭ B♭ D♭

G9

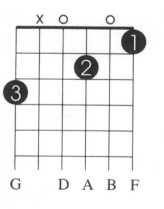
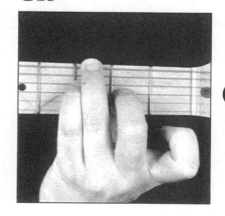

G D A B F

G13

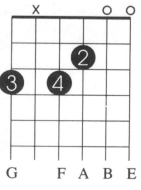

G F A B E

Gmaj7

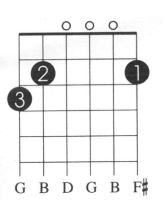

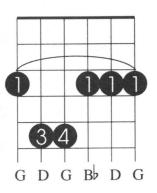

G B D G B F#

Gm7

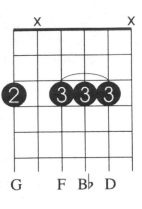

G F Bb D

Gm

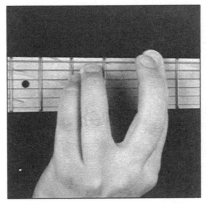

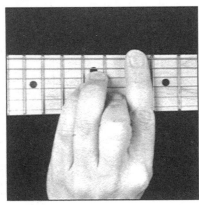

G D G Bb D G

Gm

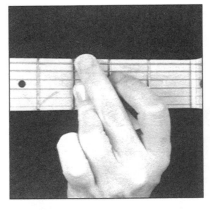

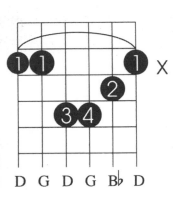

D G D G Bb D

Gm6

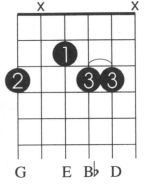

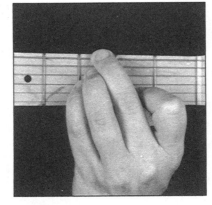

G E Bb D

Gm7b5

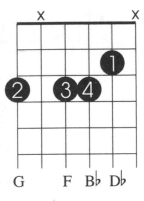

G F Bb Db

Gm(maj7)

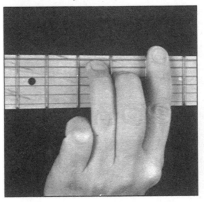

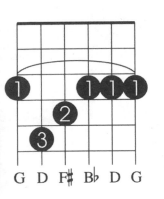

G D F# Bb D G

Gm11

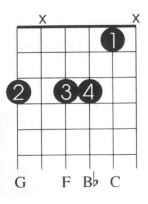

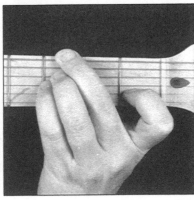

G F Bb C

A♭/G♯ chords

A♭ major

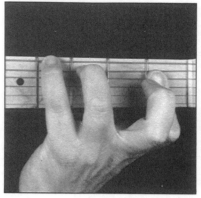
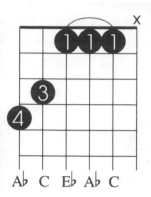

A♭ C E♭ A♭ C

A♭ major

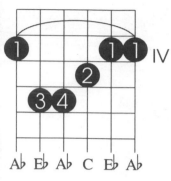
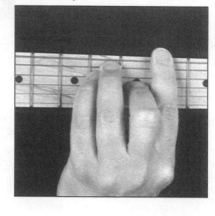

IV

A♭ E♭ A♭ C E♭ A♭

A♭sus4

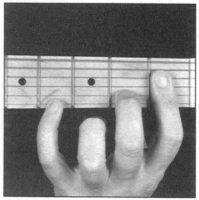
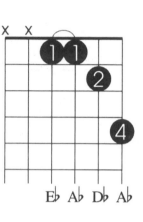

E♭ A♭ D♭ A♭

A♭6

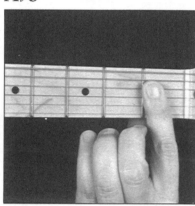
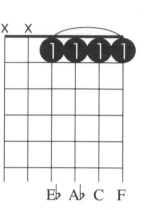

E♭ A♭ C F

A♭7

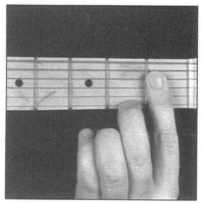
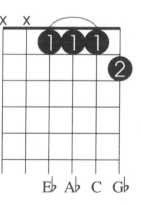

E♭ A♭ C G♭

A♭°7

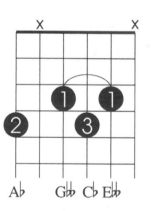
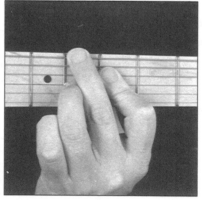

A♭ G♭♭ C♭ E♭♭

A♭9

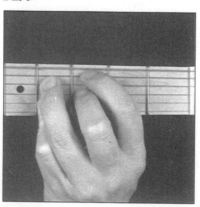
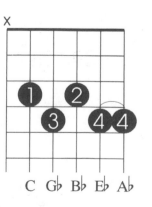

C G♭ B♭ E♭ A♭

A♭13

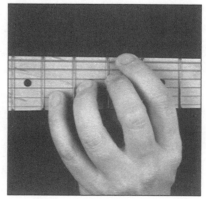
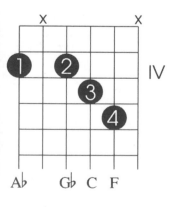

IV

A♭ G♭ C F

A♭maj7

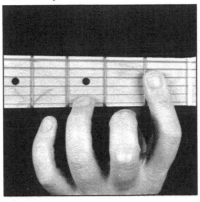

x x

| | | ① | ① | ① | |
| 3 |

E♭ A♭ C G

A♭m7

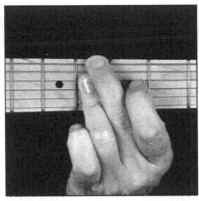

x x x

② ③ ③ ③ — IV

A♭ G♭ C♭ E♭

A♭m

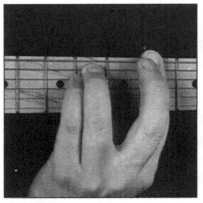

| ① | | ① | ① | ① | — IV |
| ③ | ④ |

A♭ E♭ A♭ C♭ E♭ A♭

A♭m

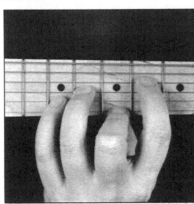

x x

| ① | | |
| | | ② | — VI |
| ③ |
| ④ |

A♭ E♭ A♭ C♭

A♭m6

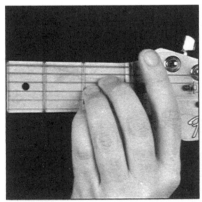

x x ○

② ③ ④

E♭ A♭ C♭ F

A♭m7♭5

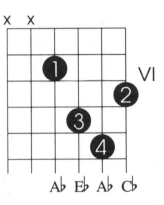

x x

| ① | | |
| ③ ③ ③ | — VI |

A♭ E♭♭ G♭ C♭

A♭m(maj7)

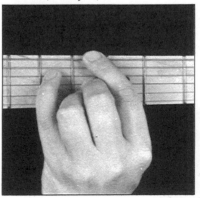

x x

① ② ③
④

A♭ G C♭ E♭

A♭m11

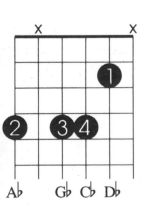

x x

| | | | ① |
| ② | ③ ④ |

A♭ G♭ C♭ D♭

25

A chords

A major

(○) ○   ○
② ① ③

E A E A C# E

A major

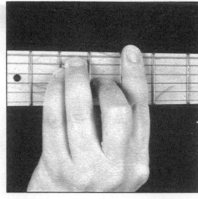

①   ① ① V
   ②
③ ④

A E A C# E A

Asus4

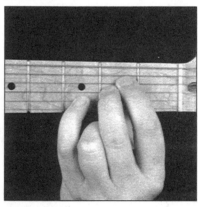

(○) ○   ○
① ②
   ④

E A E A D E

A6

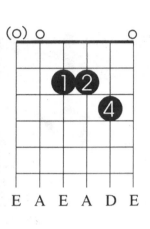
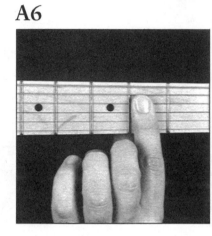

(○) ○
① ① ① ①

E A E A C# F#

A7

(○) ○
① ① ①
   ②

E A E A C# G

A°7

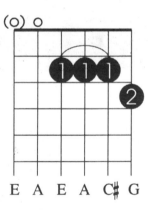
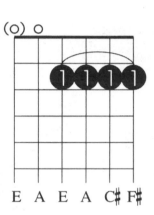

x ○
①   ②
③   ④

A E♭ A C G♭

A9

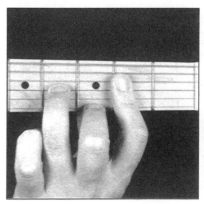

x ○
① ①
   ②
③

A E B C# G

A13

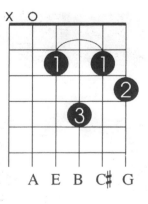
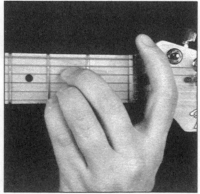
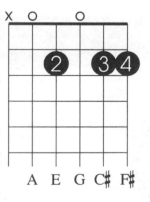
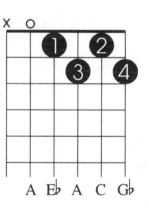

x ○   ○
② ③ ④

A E G C# F#

Amaj7

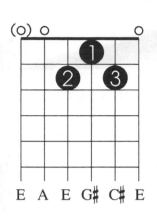

E A E G# C# E

Am7

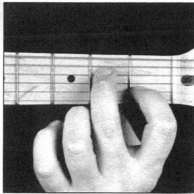
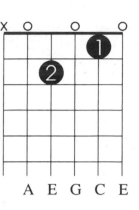

A E G C E

Am

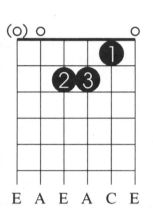

E A E A C E

Am

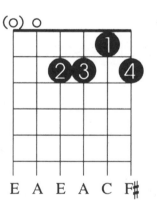
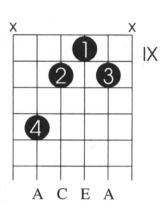

IX

A C E A

Am6

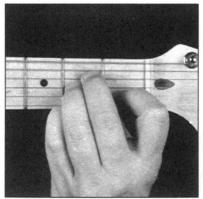
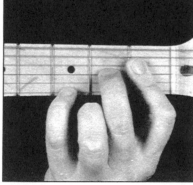

E A E A C F#

Am7♭5

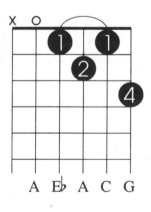

A E♭ A C G

Am(maj7)

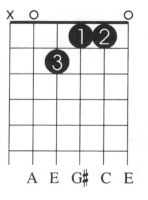

A E G# C E

Am11

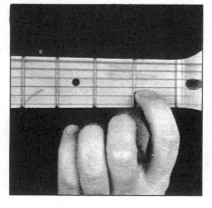

A D G C E

B♭/A♯ chords

B♭ major

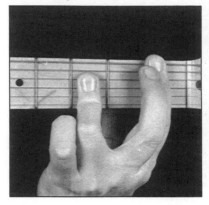

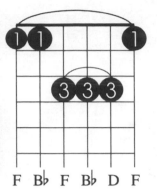

F B♭ F B♭ D F

B♭ major

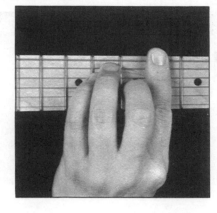

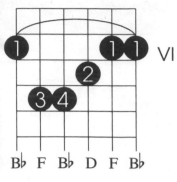

VI

B♭ F B♭ D F B♭

B♭sus4

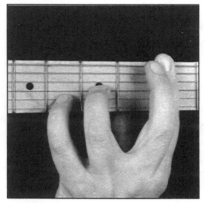

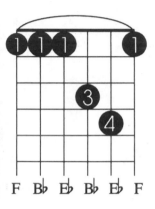

F B♭ E♭ B♭ E♭ F

B♭6

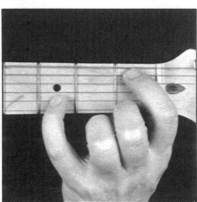

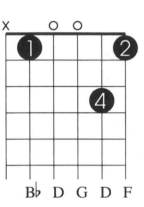

B♭ D G D F

B♭7

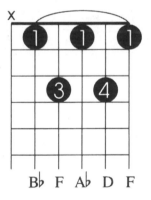

B♭ F A♭ D F

B♭°7

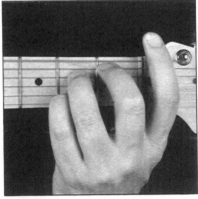

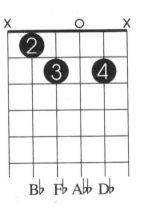

B♭ F♭ A♭♭ D♭

B♭9

B♭ D A♭ C F

B♭13

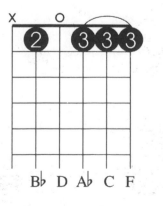

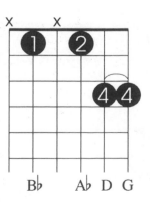

B♭ A♭ D G

B♭maj7

B♭ F A D F

B♭m7

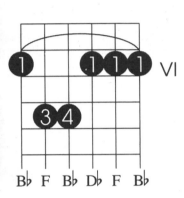

F B♭ F A♭ D♭ F

B♭m

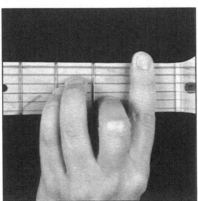

F B♭ F B♭ D♭ F

B♭m

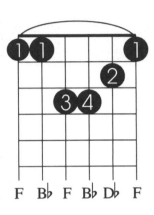

VI

B♭ F B♭ D♭ F B♭

B♭m6

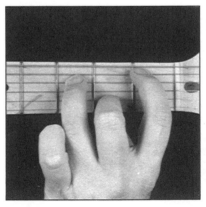

B♭ F G D♭

B♭m7♭5

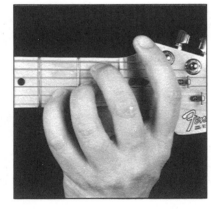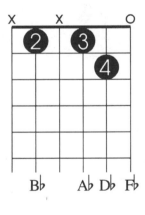

B♭ A♭ D♭ F♭

B♭m(maj7)

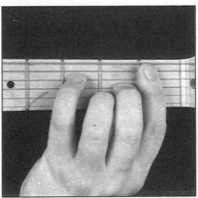

B♭ F A D♭ F

B♭m11

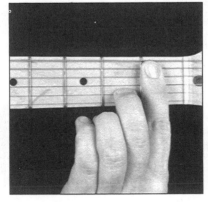

B♭ E♭ A♭ D♭ F

B chords

B major

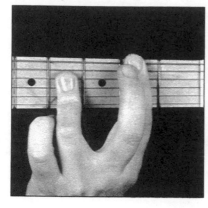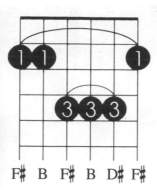

F# B F# B D# F#

B major

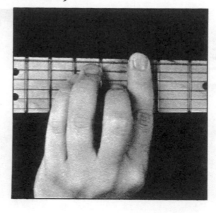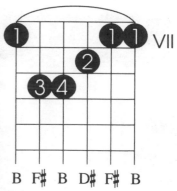

VII

B F# B D# F# B

Bsus4

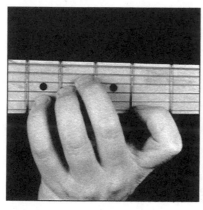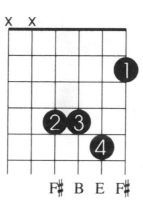

x x

F# B E F#

B6

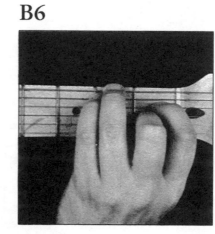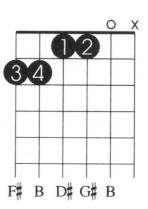

O x

F# B D# G# B

B7

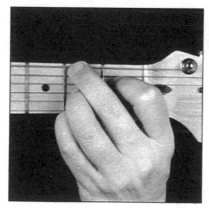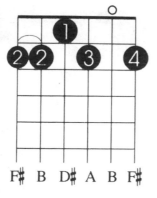

O

F# B D# A B F#

B°7

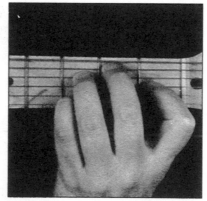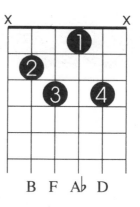

x x

B F Ab D

B9

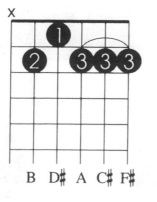

x

B D# A C# F#

B13

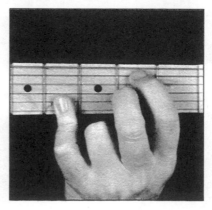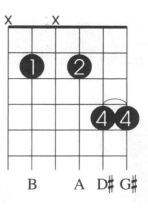

x x

B A D# G#

Bmaj7

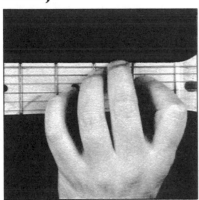
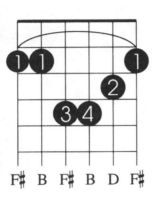

F# B D# A# B

Bm7

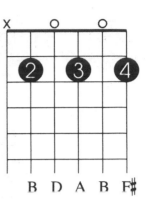
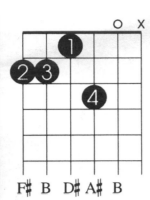

B D A B F#

Bm

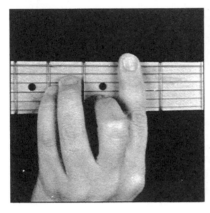
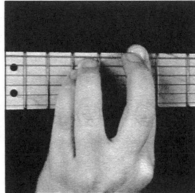

F# B F# B D F#

Bm

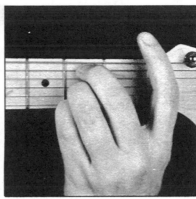
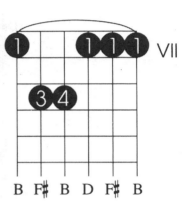

VII

B F# B D F# B

Bm6

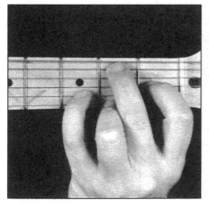
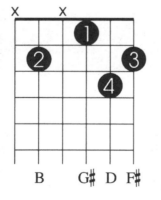

B G# D F#

Bm7♭5

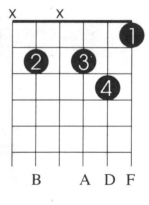
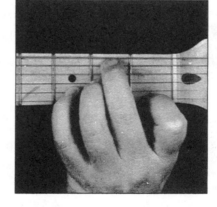

B A D F

Bm(maj7)

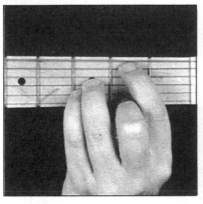
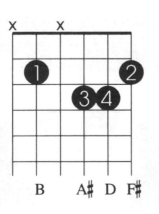

B A# D F#

Bm11

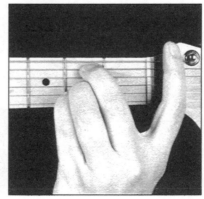

B D A C# E

Special Chords

The chords forms below are know as *5 chords* or *power chords*. These forms are most commonly used in rock, but you will find uses for them in other styles as well.

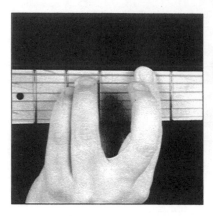 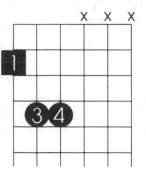 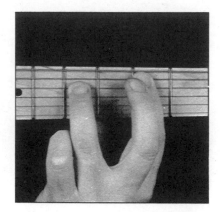 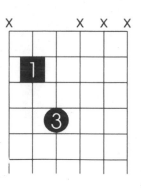

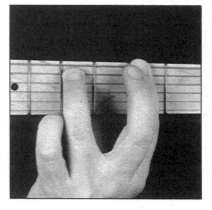 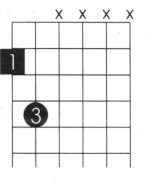 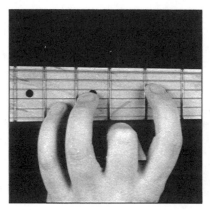 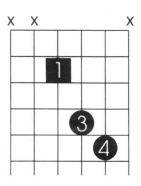

These forms are major and minor triads constructed on the first three strings.

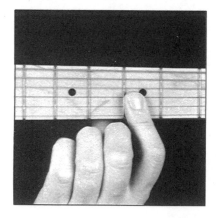 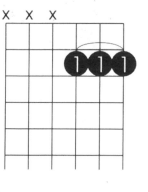 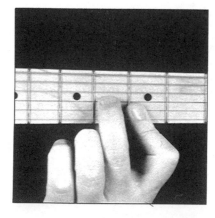 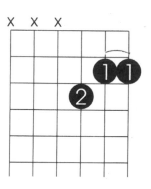

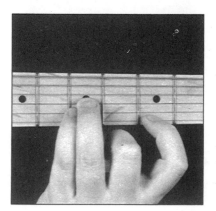 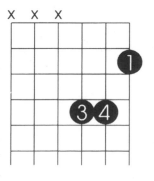 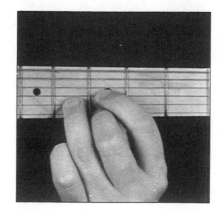 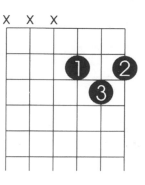